ALL DRESSED UP AND NO PLACE TO GO

WELCOME TO SUBURBIA

IS THIS REALITY?

D0583127

I'VE LOST MY KEYS,
LOST MY MONEY,
AND NOW I'VE GONE
AND LOST MY **MIND**!

The Lost Generation

For Cleo

By air mail
Par avion

POSTCARD

First published in
Great Britain in 1985
by Sidgwick & Jackson Ltd.

ISBN **0-283-99304-9**
©COPYRIGHT 1985 CHIC PIX
PRINTED IN GREAT BRITAIN

Sidgwick & Jackson Ltd,
1 Tavistock Chambers,
Bloomsbury Way,
London WC1A 2SG

Book Design by Chic Pix

Chic Pix

I WALKED WITH A ZOMBIE

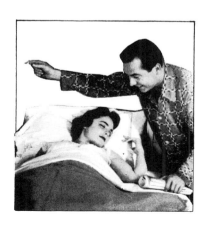

SIDGWICK & JACKSON
LONDON

IF MEN WORE PRICE TAGS

(Man's New Servant, the Friendly Atom)

SO FAR, SO GOOD

Smartest of

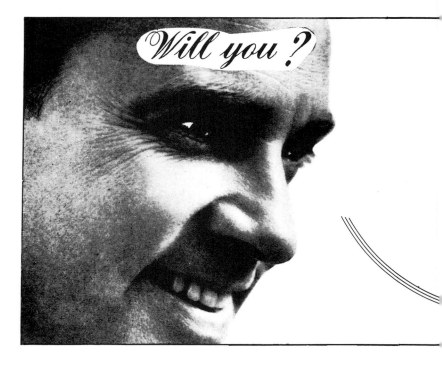

Will you ?

HAVE A NON — SEXIST NON — RACIST

the Smart

WHY YES, I'D LOVE TO!

NON   HIERARCHICAL   RELATIONSHIP

"nuclear energy"

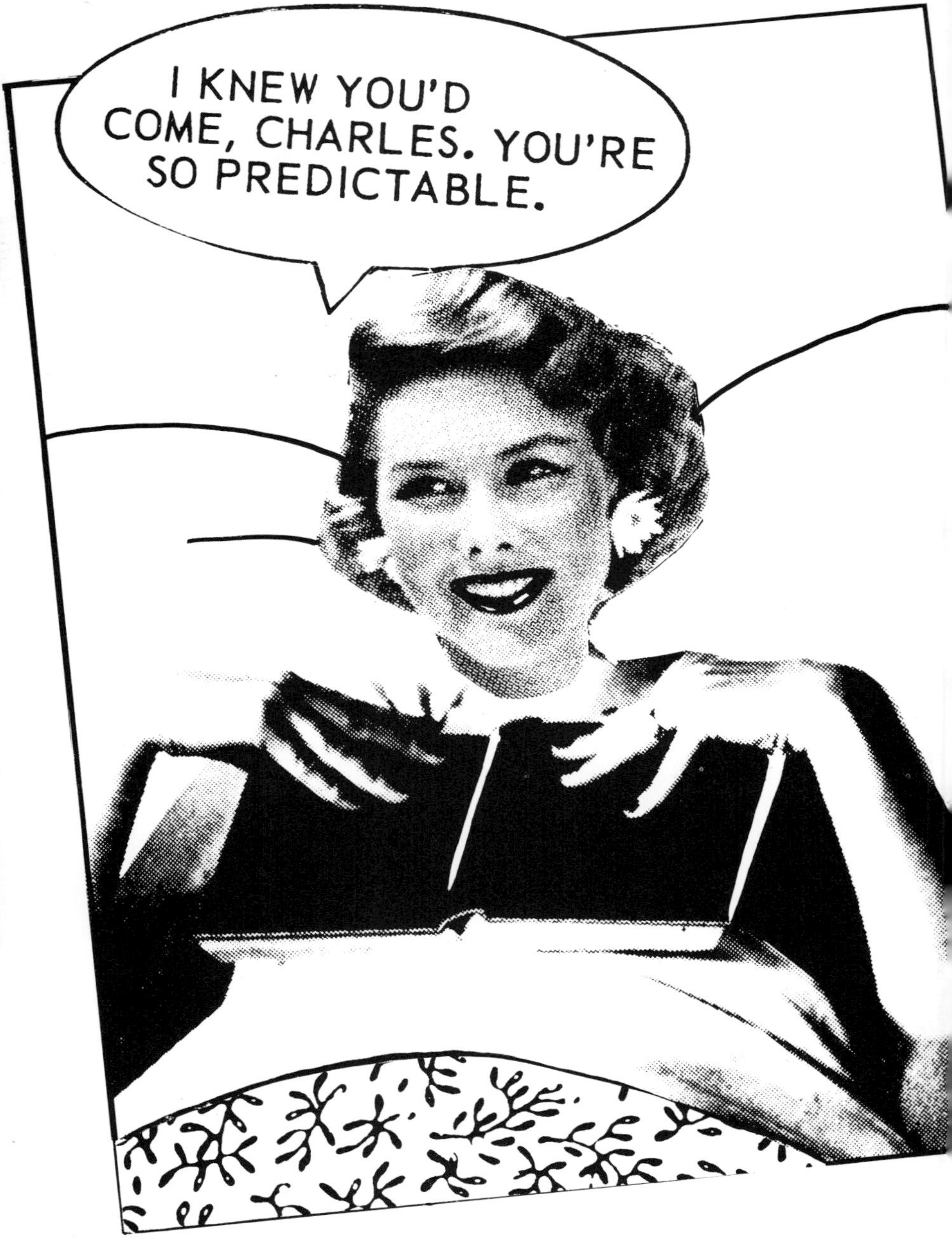

Thank You For

a Lovely Evening

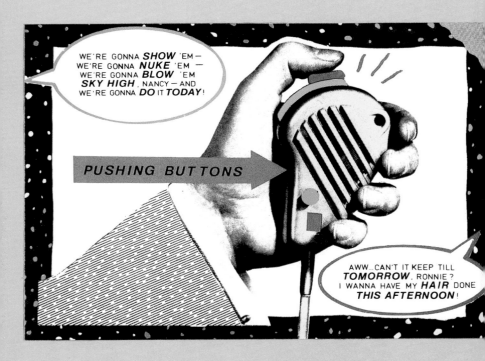

Who Says
It's a
Woman's World?

12 STARTLING SECRETS TO A MORE BEAUTIFUL BUST

WHAT MAKES MEN TICK? Understand Physiology and Psychology of the Male Sex

DATING, NECKING, 25 Guidelines to Personal Success

15 WAYS TO ACT SOPHISTICATED AND SMOOTH WITH MEN:

A GIRL TRYING TO DECIDE ABOUT A CAREER, OR MARRIAGE IS FACED WITH MANY BEWILDERING PROBLEMS. THESE GUIDES OFFER STARTLING YET SENSIBLE INFORMATION.

"Perfect Impression!"

REMEMBER
Plutonium blasts
take place in
a fraction
of a second.

MAKE IT AN OUT OF THIS WORLD XMAS

Trap
of
L-O-V-E

AFTER THE MEAL THEY WENT TO THE CINEMA, THEN KEITH TOOK HER HOME.
Y-YOU MEAN ME, MR. MANNING? WHAT SORT OF FAVOR?
Career girl B-l-u-e-s

Go Sight-Seeing
IN
London

HERE'S LOOKING AT YOU, KID!

LATER, DENISE GOT THROUGH
TO THE LADIES' SINGLES FINAL

ABOUT THE AUTHORS

Peta Coplans and Stanley Becker are Chic Pix. Their obsession is with the Fifties — the decade in which Plastic finally triumphed.

They work in London. Their video "Images by Chic Pix" was shown on Channel Four and in the U.S.A. by the Public Broadcasting Services.

Their work has been exhibited in Paris, Amsterdam and London.